ARE WE HAPPY YET?

Lisa Cypers Kamen

ARE WE HAPPY YET?

**Eight Keys to Unlocking
a Joyful Life**

LANGDON STREET PRESS

MINNEAPOLIS, MN

Langdon Street Press
212 3rd Avenue North, Suite 290
Minneapolis, MN 55401
612.455.2293
www.langdonstreetpress.com

ISBN-13: 978-1-936782-97-0
LCCN: 2012934294

Distributed by Itasca Books

Cover Design and Typeset by Sophie Chi

Printed in the United States of America

Disclaimer

The purpose of this book is to educate, delight, provoke, and entertain. Its contents are not a substitute for medical, clinical, or psychological treatment. Neither the author nor the publisher guarantees the outcome of the tips, techniques, or information contained herein, and they have neither liability nor responsibility to anyone for any claim of loss or damage caused or alleged to be caused, directly or indirectly, by the information contained in this book.

For my children, Kayla and Aryel,
who consistently teach me where happiness lives daily,
and for Chris, who proved that the sun does in fact
always shine after the storm

Ding-dong. Your joy awaits. Answer the bell.

Table of Contents

Chapter 8

Foreword

I first met Lisa Kamen at my home in Portland, Oregon. She arrived on a typically rainy afternoon, with her daughter and camera equipment in tow. Lisa was in the midst of realizing a dream: she was making a movie about happiness. In a world where everyone from my postal worker to the guy at the deli seems to have an idea for a screenplay, it was refreshing to see Lisa making this dream a reality. What's more, she was using this extraordinary opportunity as a means of showing her daughter the world. Lisa was traveling around the United States and abroad, asking people about their happiness. As a happiness researcher myself, I believe that Lisa's work is both important and instructive.

Make no mistake: I sometimes feel a degree of territoriality that comes with professional expertise. Like many academics, I can feel my feathers getting ruffled when someone comes along and offers her armchair view on the complicated architecture of happiness. It is, however, people exactly like Lisa who have turned around my attitude. In every subsequent meeting with Lisa, I have been reminded of her deep well of humanity—donating money to schools, serving others, doting on her children, and helping our returning soldiers and their families, challenged by combat stress, restore their smiles and thrive through Harvesting

Happiness for Heroes. I have come to realize that voices like Lisa's are not just tolerable in the public conversation on happiness but welcome. By virtue of her media—film and popular writing—and through her breadth of experience, Lisa offers new insights into living the Good Life.

Many of these ideas you will—fortunately—find in the pages of this book. To name just a single example, Lisa does a clever job of describing the relationship between "having more" and "having less" of a commodity, such as time or money. She throws conventional thinking to the wind and offers a more complex view of these psychological leanings. It is not that having more is better and having less is worse. Lisa challenges us all to look at the balancing act between more and less. I will leave it for you to discover in the pages ahead exactly how to do this. This book is full of these types of gems, and I hope you are as affected by Lisa's positive contribution to the world as I am.

Dr. Robert Biswas-Diener
Managing Director, Positive Acorn
Portland, Oregon
September 21, 2011

Introduction

If I were to ask you what makes you happy, would you be able to answer? Don't worry if you couldn't. You're not the only one who's struggling right now to find your happiness without quite knowing what it looks like. All you know is this: things aren't right, and you need to do something about it.

You might be thinking that you've already done everything you were supposed to do to be happy: you played by the rules, you went to school, you got married, you had kids. But no matter what you attained or what you achieved, you just felt like something was missing—and you realized you didn't know what it was or how to find it.

So you did the things everyone else did to make themselves happy: you bought new things, read books, watched movies, took classes, went to the gym, lost weight.

And still, you weren't happy.

Or maybe you built your company, married a beautiful woman, and now drive the car of your childhood dreams, but every day, you still wake up with the feeling that there should be something more to your life.

I know how this feels. I've been there. Things would be so much easier if achieving the American dream would fulfill us inside. If things really happened the way they do in the movies.

But what happens after the credits fade?
What does happily ever after actually look like?

We, as humans, may be shaped by our pasts, but we do not have to be defined by them. Our emotional baggage can be our greatest enemy or serve as our most helpful catalyst for transformation. Since I began working in the business of happiness in 2007, I have witnessed tremendous uncertainty, changes, and growth in my own life, both personally and professionally.

My desire to serve others in their quest to create a thriving life is how I have chosen to transform my own adversity into greater happiness and well-being. I've found that when there is an alignment of passion, purpose, place, and meaning, new doors open. With the right tools, the life force within all of us can be released. I'm living proof that the eight keys to unlocking a joyful life work—I use each and every one of them and, as a result, thrive, rather than merely survive, through each day.

The intention behind this book is to debunk the "smiley face" notion of happiness. Happiness isn't an icon that you insert at the end of a sentence. It is a way of life, a flourishing existence defined by fulfillment, growth, and contentment. It isn't instant, and it doesn't have to be fleeting. It requires hard work. But so does anything worth having.

This book isn't a scholarly tome (intentionally so). It's a quick read, written in layperson terms for the "normies," although it is all grounded in science. Every story has a story. I did not wander into my happy place. There was a personal evolution to my happiness revolution. One does not reach the light without having traveled through the dark.

I realize there is value in sharing my story and will include it, along with the scientific theories that are the foundation of my work.

In this book, I hope you will find your answers—the keys that will help you unlock the happiness you have always desired.

Are We Happy Yet? is all about the transformative power of self-mastery. Enjoy the journey.

Lisa Cypers Kamen

1. Everyone Has A Story

As a chic, savvy, yet unhappy-inside urban mom, I set out to discover my "purpose" by enrolling in a graduate studies program in psychology, where I would produce a documentary film as my final thesis project. I wanted to create a film that would show others what my life was like *before* I started to ask myself the hard questions and how it transformed *after* I asked them.

It wasn't easy.

I wanted to stay in the same place I'd always been in. I didn't want to "rock the boat" or do anything that might cause others to think I was having some sort of crisis. But something needed to change. I knew I wasn't happy. I knew it deep down. But what did I even know about how to attain true happiness?

As a quintessential trophy wife ensconced in a busy, bold, and chaotic life filled with two beautiful children, a seemingly loving husband (I say seemingly because sadly, our relationship later disintegrated), a large network of friends and family, travel, fashion, jewelry, cars, and homes, I had it all. Yet none of it was enough. On the outside, I was living a "happy life," but internally, I lacked authentic, meaningful joy.

I was thirsting for change and determined to educate and grow myself to create a more peaceful, meaningful, and contented life. After so many years of building a warm, nurturing home, raising children, and cultivating a marriage, it had been a long time since I had taken the time to think about myself and my own happiness. I was parched from the years of focusing on everyone else.

I had a hunch that true and sustainable happiness would become available to me upon my realization of a greater sense of passion, purpose, place, and meaning. After all, that's what all the self-help gurus would always say: if you find your passion, you'll find your happiness. I believed it. So, at the tender age of forty-one, I went back to school to simultaneously complete the last year of my bachelor's degree in architectural design studies and the first year of my graduate degree in psychology.

You might ask what architecture and psychology have in common. Most people might answer "Nothing," but these two subjects were my passions, and I wanted to make them blend together. And they do.

Architecture is about designing physical space, and psychology is about organizing mental worlds. Still, while I might have been able to create a structure for a house, creating my own inner framework did not seem as easy as drawing up a blueprint. What I did know was that I was determined to figure out how to create a new, better life for myself and the people in my life (especially my kids) who would be affected by my return to school so late in the game.

It was a daunting task to attempt two academic years at once. As a young college student straight out of high school, I probably would not have taken this on. But for me, at forty-one, I realized I had nothing to lose and everything to gain. It was time to stop worrying so much about what I *couldn't* do. No longer would I just wander from one thing to the next, trying to find a way to satisfy my desire for "something." That doesn't mean I wasn't afraid from time to time; I was. But I also knew I was on the right track to getting my life back in order.

My initial goal was to complete my graduate studies and become a traditional counseling psychologist, seeing patients in a classic one-on-one office setting. I envisioned my clients coming in with their problems and walking out with solutions. I would come up with a brilliant answer, and suddenly they would be happy. I imagined hugs and gratitude. I imagined having my own questions answered through the patients I saw. Just like on television, I would discover the key to my own happiness because of my work.

Soon after I began my master's program, I realized I did not have the patience to sit within the confines of an office, day in and day out, hour after hour, listening to other people's problems; this conventional setting was not a good fit for me.

That was a wake-up call.

I was dedicating myself to a program when I already knew I couldn't follow through with it. Did that mean I had wasted all of my time and money on a silly dream?

Did this mean that happiness was even farther away than I'd thought it to be?

Was this just *another* example of how my big dreams were nothing more than illusions?

Of course not. It was all part of my journey.

 *Key One*

We all have a story to tell. Regardless of our personal histories, a good life really is available to all of us, no matter where we come from. It is essential that we understand that suffering is just a natural part of life. It need not define who we are or keep us from joy.

Personal stories. We all have them, don't we? If you look around your local bookstore, you'll notice a recurring genre in the bestsellers—memoirs. Sharing our stories can be liberating, especially when they inspire others.

But our stories can become our prisons, too.

When we continue to tell ourselves that we are defined by a certain experience or that there is only a certain future story that we are destined to live, we limit who we are.

Think about your last job and how that ended. If it ended badly, you probably were nervous about your next job, thinking about whether you were going to have the same experience in your new role. You played your old story in your head, but sometimes, just thinking about these other stories is enough to cause them to repeat themselves.

"Our past is a story existing only in our minds. Look, analyze, understand, and forgive. Then, as quickly as possible, chuck it."

—*Marianne Williamson*

What we forget sometimes—well, what we forget *often*—is that the stories that *have* happened to us are not the stories that *will* happen to us. The stories people tell us about how things *should be* or how things *have always been* are just that: stories. They are not facts. They are not guaranteed. They are merely options.

Stories, whether they are our own or the stories of those around us, can inspire or destroy. Although they can uplift us when they are positive, they can be even more destructive when they are not. When stories fail to teach something new, or if they just remind us of things we regret and cannot change, these stories hold us back.

Think about the stories you tell yourself. Indeed, you probably have many. You tell yourself these stories because you think they are important. But if they don't contribute to your happiness, it's time to do what Marianne Williamson says to do: chuck them.

Because the stories you tell yourself should empower you, not hold you back.

True happiness is born of experience, not of ignorance. Embrace the experiences you are dealt—even when they are negative. Sometimes, it is only after weathering a storm that we understand what true happiness really feels and looks like. Take what you can of the negative experiences, and then let them go; let them pass over you like a warm breeze on a summer night.

In the 1993 film *Shadowlands*, the main character, Jack, illustrates this point when he says, "Why love, if losing hurts so much? I have no answers anymore, only the life I have lived. Twice in that life I've been given the choice: as a boy and as a man. The boy chose safety; the man chooses suffering. The pain now is part of the happiness then. That's the deal."

Let me take you back to a scorching-hot day while I was bicycling in northern India. That's right. Picture me as my former princess self, biking in the 110-degree heat in Rajasthan near the Pakistan border.

"Lucky" is the word that drifted in and out of my mind as I traveled the bumpy roads. I was far away from my world—and intentionally so. This was my first chance in years to be away from my children and spouse. I was grateful for the opportunity to explore myself in an environment so different from my own. I was able to take a break from my old stories for a bit. By removing myself from the way things *were* in my life, I hoped to find out how they *could be* when I returned.

For a few years prior to my visit, my former husband and I had donated money to the Sulaxmi School for Girls in Lucknow, India, to support students who normally would not have access to even basic education. These were children of the streets, many of whom called a tarp strung between two trees "home" and had never been to school. The school's mission was and is to give these girls a fundamental education. Learning reading, writing, and arithmetic would enable them to later work and be more independent. Although the education they received at the school was basic, it was far more than they had ever been given, and it allowed them to work to bring money to their families and into their villages. This small change in their lives could rescue girls from a life on the streets or the fate of an arranged childhood marriage. The school made me hopeful. By supporting it, I knew I was doing something important for the girls I helped and for future generations.

On this life-altering trip to India, I brought a small video camera, with the intention of making a small promotional piece about the Sulaxmi School to raise money for it upon my return to the States. I wanted to capture the simplicity of its mission: to educate a generation of girls so the cycle of poverty could be broken. What I didn't realize at the time was that as I helped these girls, I also helped myself, changing the course of my life.

From this profound experience I learned a powerful lesson: nothing is impossible.

Think about that for a moment. *Nothing is impossible.*

Although we tend to focus on what isn't possible in our lives, the truth is that we are powerful, manifesting creatures. In the numerous villages I visited throughout India, where they lacked even basic essentials for life and growth, happiness existed and life was thriving. In these villages, I experienced joy that wasn't rooted in possessions.

I learned that one person can make a difference in the lives of many. And this was a lesson that resonated in my bones. I thought about how ripples in the water begin with the slightest touch on the water's surface. I thought about the way that I would be touching the area with my video and my voice.

By believing in myself, I could change the world around me. I could grow and stretch beyond my wildest expectations. Because I helped these girls, their expectations for themselves and for their futures grew. They were no longer limited by the stories they were born into and what they thought was going to happen to them. And neither was I.

As I rode through the Indian countryside, a bright-eyed, glaringly obvious Western tourist, I observed the beautiful nature of India's people—friendly, warm, inviting, and happy, despite the poverty surrounding them. What was the mysterious ingredient that allowed their joyful, inner light to radiate out through their eyes for all to see?

Today, think about your personal story and the stories you tell yourself:

- What stories do you tell yourself again and again?

- What happens when you live within the stories you tell?

- What might happen if you decided to stop telling yourself old stories?

- What would happen if you rewrote your personal stories?

- Name ways in which past suffering has helped you in your present life (e.g., you're stronger, more resilient, more confident, less willing to take abuse from others).

Sustainable happiness exists regardless of scarcity or abundance, regardless of poverty or wealth, and regardless of external circumstance. Want to know why? Because happiness is an inside job!

Notes to Self:

2. Letting Your Inner child Light The Way

Just for a moment, stop and think about your day. Did you laugh today (even if only for a moment)? Probably not as much as you used to. Statistics show that children laugh an average of 80 percent more per day than adults. That's because children view their world through a different lens than we do. They seek out and create joy for themselves naturally. Beyond that, children laugh unconditionally— they don't allow external or internal negativity to impact their appreciation of joyful moments when they arise. Children are naturally curious and filled with wonder about life.

Instead of worrying about everything that could possibly go wrong, children believe that life is exciting and happy. Why do they think this way? Because they aren't weighed down by the stories adults tell themselves. They don't stop to think about the past; they simply do what brings them joy in the moment and are rewarded with happiness and laughter.

I know what you're thinking. *"But Lisa, they're just kids. They don't have a care in the world. No mortgage; no awareness of war and sickness. Of course they are happy!"* But kids are aware. They recognize the struggle. Have you noticed how children don't have filters? They'll just tell you what they think. And they have opinions about everything, including all the negative, difficult things we try our best to shield them from. The difference is their outlook: they are open, hopeful, and optimistic. They aren't jaded or hindered by their stories the way adults are. It is the stories we tell ourselves that oftentimes hide the joy that is right in front of us.

It comes down to **spontaneity** and **responsibility**. When we are young and carefree, we simply take each moment as it comes, enjoy it, and then seek out another to replace it. We don't go back and forth about how things *could* be better. We focus on the moment we are in and make the most of it. Even if that means fashioning a toy out of a ball of string instead of having an expensive Barbie doll or toy car.

It isn't until we start school and board the "Achievement Express" to college that we begin to feel the weight of responsibility and expectation and obligation and excess. We become aware of—and oftentimes dwell on—our weaknesses, and we start doing things because we want to fit in, instead of doing things to make ourselves happy. We become less invested in the moment and more consumed with the future. Everyone starts to ask, *"What do you want to be when you grow up?"* and if we don't know, or if we have the *wrong* answer, we start to question our self-worth.

Oh, how quickly the pleasure of childhood disappears.

In order to be "successful" adults, we need to be more resolute, more serious, and more somber. We can't "waste" our time playing, laughing, simply being happy. We have more important things to take care of. Our to-do lists keep growing longer, our need to impress others becomes all encompassing, and we settle for being what everyone else thinks we should be.

It's no wonder that we can't seem to be spontaneous anymore.

You've probably found yourself in the situation where someone has asked you to take a step off your perfectly constructed path, a step you hadn't anticipated taking. Maybe it's a matter of taking an impromptu trip to a new country or getting involved in a volunteer organization that would cut into your weekends at work. Even though you could have participated (and maybe even secretly wanted to participate) in these unexpected opportunities, you didn't. The thought of a change in plans—especially one that would take you away from work—stressed you out, so you passed on it.

And then you regretted your decision. When it was too late.

The truth is that we all have responsibilities. We will always have one more thing to cross off our to-do lists.

But that doesn't mean we can't take advantage of unexpected opportunities, while smiling every step of the way.

Where have all your smiles gone? Have you tucked them away for certain people or for certain occasions? Have you decided that smiling makes you look immature or somehow ignorant of the realities of your oh-so-serious life?

There are smiles that are aching to be released from your body. Why are you holding them back?

While happy times are certainly good times to smile, they are not the only times. When you release an unexpected smile, you show the world that happiness and joy are possible—at *any time*. You remind yourself that happiness is tenable, even when times are hard and your life feels dark.

In truth, it's actually more important to laugh during difficult times than happy ones because laughter is a release. It breaks up tension. It helps you breathe. Think about a time when you were consoling a friend who lost a loved one. At first, you grieve with them. You cry. You comfort. But then, you make a joke and your friend laughs for the first time in days. And you laugh with them.

And didn't that feel great? Perhaps the laughter helps the situation more than the tears?

Key Two

Have a chat with your inner child—you know, the spontaneous one who doesn't care what everyone else thinks and hasn't become jaded by the harsh realities of your adult life. This little one knows exactly where your happiness is hidden.

You only need to remember that your inner child is just as smart—if not smarter than—the adult version of you, because it is the most authentic version of you. By tapping into your inner child, you create a connection between your true self and the self that you've been presenting to the world for the past ten, twenty, or even thirty or more years. The best part? Your inner child knows exactly where you've concealed your happiness.

Like any good investigator, ask your inner child some questions to see what he wants and needs to be happy. Don't worry if this is difficult at first. It's like reconnecting with an old friend: things may be a little awkward at first, but once you start talking, you'll instantly remember why you connected in the first place.

Start by asking your inner child:

- What makes you happy?

- Would having *more* make you happy?

- What do you want to try that you haven't tried before?

- What have you done in the past to be happy that might look a little silly as an adult? (Do it anyway!)

These are simple questions—questions you might have skipped over in the past because you thought you already knew the answers. But until you ask your inner child these questions, chances are you really don't know the answers after all. Because when you ask your inner child, your answers won't be hindered by the stories you've told yourself or what society considers to be the "right" answers. Because this isn't about what *should* make you happy: this is about finding out what *actually* makes you happy, *right now.*

What makes you smile? What makes you excited? What makes you want to jump up and down with enthusiasm? What makes your heart sing? When we cultivate our intuition by asking and answering these fundamental questions of our inner child, we attain greater joy because we are better aligned with our true character.

So stop contemplating what others think. Instead of finding answers externally, look within yourself. Because the journey to happiness isn't about everyone else. This journey is about *you.*

Notes to Self:

3. When Less Is More

The quest for more. The thing that controls all of our lives.

What's interesting is that we think that the people who have just a few more perks than we do—a better job, a higher salary, a bigger house—are the ones who never have to worry about anything.

We perceive that they have it all.

But of course, oftentimes they don't. Because when it comes to the theory of "more," things aren't always what they appear to be. So when we see people who have more than we have, we wonder why they aren't happier. We wonder why they're not smiling from ear to ear. If you've noticed this track in the theory of "more," you're already aware that things aren't always what they appear to be.

More money, more fame, more power, more time, more stuff, more sex, more food, more wine, more Xanax, more sleep, more vacation, more friends, more connections—none of it will do the trick. You can have it all and still be unhappy.

Think of this as a bowl of water with a hole in it. No matter how many times you try to fill it up, the hole still leaks, and the bowl never gets filled. Though you may try to fill it again and again, something is preventing you from the fullness that you seek.

Deep down, you already know this. You know that having more isn't a solution. If it were, there would be a point at which you would have enough, and you would just be happy, right?

But having enough and just being happy isn't what we are taught. From an early age, we're taught that happiness depends on owning more stuff—from children's toys, like dolls and trucks, to adult toys, like expensive jewelry and sports cars. But who benefits from this way of living: us or the sellers of so-called happiness packaged in the form of consumer goods?

Key Three

More is not better. Most of the time, it's just more! Focus on enjoying your journey, not attaining more stuff.

When you look at the items you own, the places you've been, the relationships you've developed, and the experiences you've had, what sticks out as being the most important and valuable part of your life? Is it the things you own?

Probably not. And yet, we spend a lot of time and energy focused on attaining and achieving things.

The concept and the illusion of "more" can be likened to a carrot at the end of a stick. No matter how fast you run, that carrot will always be out of reach. You will do everything you can, forgetting about everything else, because you want that one "carrot," even though it becomes clear you will never have it.

You will never reach the ideal amount of "more" because there *isn't* an ideal amount. Sure, the stores and the advertisements might try to make you believe that if you buy the one item they are pushing—the carrot they dangle in front of you—your life will be complete, and you will be happy. But of course, that's not true. Whatever product they're pushing is just the "gateway drug." You'll never actually get the sense of satisfaction you secretly hope the carrot represents.

What if you began to focus less on the carrot and more on the journey? What if you began to think about how to make the journey more fun? More relaxing? More inspired? More connected and more present? What if you began to walk instead of run and started to look around you instead of at the carrot. In time, you might realize that although someone or something will always be dangling a carrot in front of you, it doesn't have to be the only point of your journey.

By focusing on your journey instead, you might even stop reaching for the carrot completely and realize how much you already have. And when you do, an amazing feeling will creep up all around you. (Hint: it's your happiness.) While you were focusing on your journey instead of the carrot, your happiness developed naturally along the way.

Let's look at the other side of more: less. When did less become such a horrible thing? And what are we comparing it to? Less than what? Perhaps we've linked "less" to things that are supposed to be important to us:

- Less time

- Less money

- Less happiness

But when we think about "more," we can see how "more" is causing just as much anxiety as "less" ever could.

- With less time, we have more worries. With more responsibilities, we have less time.

- With more money, we have less time and often less happiness.

- With less happiness, we spend more money and have less time because we need to work more to pay for the things that were supposed to make us happier.

Getting dizzy yet? The truth is that everything is interconnected in some way, and how we decide to act is oftentimes driven entirely by our perspective. If we think that having "more" will lead to happiness, we will pursue "more," regardless of the problems "more" brings into our lives—which is dangerous, because "more" is a trick state of being.

When you have more things, you have more things to take care of. When you have more people in your life, you need to maintain more relationships. When you have more responsibilities, more things can go wrong.

So stop for a minute and think about your life with less.

What might happen if you had fewer responsibilities at home or at work? What might you do with that free time? Would you take up a new hobby? Sign up for a class? What would you do with this *space*?

If you had fewer things in your home, would you feel more open? Would you feel less cluttered and chaotic? What would you do with this *space*?

Suddenly, a world of opportunity opens up.

Here's what gets lost when you are consumed by your quest for "more": when there are already so many things cluttering your life, you reach a point where you can't make space for anything else. While life might have an unlimited capacity to accept and to give new things, you do not. You can't take on more work than can fit into twenty-four hours. You can't buy more things than what fits in your home. And when that happens, there's no room for the things you truly need to be happy. Instead, you're engulfed by the things you thought you wanted.

Maybe more isn't such a great idea.

It's no wonder that the minimalist approach is becoming popular—trendy, even. People are seeking ways to simplify their lives and to learn to live with less. And what do they find?

Those who have less in their lives actually have more:

- Financial security. They're not paying for the upkeep of a lot of things. They're not paying for a larger house or a storage facility to hold their possessions.

- They have more time to do things because they're not spending their time shopping or working too hard in order to maintain a certain lifestyle.

- Instead of focusing on that one carrot of satisfaction that is always out of reach, minimalists are able to focus on what's important—what they already have.

This isn't to say you should run out right now and divest yourself of all worldly possessions, but this is a great time to think about what you do have. Make a list of all of the things you have in your life right now, from physical possessions to relationships.

Chances are good that this list is longer than you thought it was. In fact, you might even feel self-conscious that you were even worried about not having enough. Keep this list close to you as a reminder of all the "more" you already have in your life.

Now take a step back and think about the way you have been living. Are you living a meaningful, happy existence in this very moment? Or have you been focusing on the prizes you hope to accumulate in the future, giving up days and weeks and months of potential happiness along the way?

Just checking in … are you starting to see the potential for happiness in your life?

"*A little*," you say. "*But I have real problems in my life. I have real issues. Things that make it very hard to be happy!*"

Don't worry; we're going to tackle that, too. Happiness is a complicated matter, after all. You have problems, and I have problems too.

And we can still be happy.

Notes to Self:

4. Life Is Not Always Happy (And That's Okay)

Happiness is a mysterious thing. We all want it, we all crave it, and still, we can't always have it, no matter what we do. Although advertisements try to convince us that if we take the right pill, then we can be happy all the time, but that's simply not true. Because life *isn't* always happy. This sounds harsh, but it's the truth. Happiness doesn't naturally spring up from beneath our feet each day. And that's because life isn't perfect. In fact, it can be downright cruel and unreasonable at times. And that's okay, because no matter what life throws at us, we have free will.

Stuff happens. Every second, someone is born and someone dies. Life is filled with tension, disappointment, trauma, illness, and struggle, as well as pleasure, excitement, satisfaction, beauty, and simplicity. Life is a "wiggly" experience. It moves this way and then it moves that way, often at the same time, as happiness is regularly tinged by difficulty. Life can be bittersweet.

How do you wiggle? How do you deal with the roller-coaster ride of life? How do you deal with hardships? Do you go with the flow, or do you fight the tide?

When things go wrong, do you play the victim and engage in pity parties that don't serve you? Or do you realize that you have the power to control your expectations, your reactions, your choices, and yourself?

Simply, it comes down to practicing internal control instead of external control.

What does that mean? It means we can't control the people around us, and we can't control events that happen around us. All we can control is ourselves. We can choose what we do, what we say, and most importantly, how we react. When we exercise self-control, we realize that not only are we able to create a life of happiness, but the only reason why we aren't happier right now is … well, because we're not making that choice.

You don't want to hear that, do you? No one does. But stop and think about that for a minute. The thing that's holding you back from being truly happy is … you. The hardest thing to admit? You've probably already started to realize it.

You already know that looking outside of yourself hasn't helped. You may have even tried scratching the surface of yourself to discover the cause of your unhappiness, but you stopped before digging too deeply.

And why? Because you don't want to take responsibility.

That's where you need to start fresh with a new perspective. Taking responsibility isn't about feeling bad about the choices you've made or thinking about how horrible or weak you are. It isn't about convincing yourself you are a bad person.

Stop that insanity right now. Think about this: when you realize that *you* are the one responsible for your attitudes and opinions about things not working out the way you would have liked, you will also discover that *you* have the power to change them. Reminder and fact: you are powerful beyond measure!

Yes, you're the one who can turn things around.

And when you do, the only person you'll have to "blame" for your success is *you*. And that's something to be proud of. You can stop getting in your own way by learning how to master the way you interact in the world.

The only control you truly have is over your own responses and reactions to the external world—in most cases, you can't actually control the issue you're forced to deal with. Do you think you can control the weather? Do you think you can control the government? Do you think you think you control your partner's carnal desires? (Well, maybe a little of that last one.)

Even though you may possess the best parenting skills on the planet, do you think you can control your child's destiny? Do you think you have the power to singularly stop war, famine, political despotism, or economic disaster?

Many of us truly believe that we have the power to control everything in our lives. And we think that if we just work hard enough, we'll be able to change the world around us and bend it to our will. There's this thought in our minds that we are the only ones in the universe who matter. We're the *only* ones who can do anything about what's happening around us. And that's true and untrue at the same time. Can you change your world?

The answer is **no** and **yes**. You alone cannot cure the ills of the world. You cannot declare and enforce world peace (although that would certainly be nice). But you can change yourself, and the effect of even a simple personal change can have a tremendous impact on your personal happiness and even the world. But instead of focusing on ourselves, we oftentimes try to control everything and everyone around us. We think that if we control others, we have power. And if we have power, we are happy. Right?

But total control over others is an illusion. Even if you can control what someone else does (like a parent controlling a child's schedule), you can't control how that person feels or thinks. Because no one can exert absolute control over anyone else—not even dictators. More importantly, no one likes to be controlled—not your spouse/partner, kids, friends, or coworkers. Probably not even you.

But you do have a choice: you can take control over yourself and your own life.

Key Four

We don't have control over life's circumstances, only how we relate to them.

When you focus on the big picture instead of a specific negative experience, you can stay tapped into the happiness that you have in general, instead of temporary sadness, anger, or frustration. If you think big, you can move forward. You can persevere, instead of letting your dissatisfaction bog you down and make you stagnant.

In order to be the CEO of a company, one must be resilient enough to handle all the responsibilities, stresses, and day-to-day crises that arise. Otherwise, the entire company may fall apart, because the CEO sets the tone. The CEO is the leader. Your mind is the CEO of your life. If you are unable to bounce back from a negative experience, your mind, body, and entire existence will suffer. To live a happy life, your positive capacity to cope with everyday stresses and unexpected catastrophes is instrumental.

Managing the facts and emotions of a crisis is integral to surviving it. A crisis can stir many emotions, including shock, fear, anger, action, sadness, uncertainty, despair, and even paralysis. By developing good coping strategies, one develops resiliency and the ability to gradually move forward in life to a new "normal." Coping doesn't mean ignoring your pain. It's okay to feel pain, shock, and fear. Just as a CEO will conduct a thorough assessment of his company after a negative financial quarter, you must assess your life to find the source of the negative emotions you are feeling. Find their root. Learn from them. And then let them go.

There's a great quote by Maya Angelou that sums up this fourth key perfectly:

> *"If you don't like something, change it. If you can't change it, change your attitude."*

The world is not conspiring against you, no matter what it might feel like some days. On the days when you think everyone is trying to irritate you and make things more difficult, stop and take a deep breath. Stop personalizing the behavior of others.

We live in a time when victim consciousness is prevalent. We believe that we are suffering because someone else has caused it. Continuously, we look outside of our minds and our hearts to find someone to blame. Because if we can just find someone else to blame, we don't have to take responsibility for anything. We're just victims, someone who others should pity and support.

Most of the time, however, you aren't a victim of anyone else's wrongdoing. While there are certainly moments when you might suffer at the hands of someone else, in most cases, the only person who stands in the way of your personal happiness is … well … *you.*

When you continue to blame everyone else for your missteps, you create a situation in which there is always something or someone else that prevents you from being happy. You're having a bad day? Well, your partner wasn't nice to you when you got up, so that put you in a bad mood.

And then the kids were screaming at each other, so they obviously hate you and want to make you suffer. And that brings up the good point that you're not a good parent, but that's because your parents weren't any good to you.

Can you see how this creates a cycle of blame and a cycle of trouble in your life? There will *always* be someone in your life that isn't doing what you want him or her to do. No matter how great your life is going, there will always be someone you can try to blame for not being happy. But since you can't change the way other people behave, why not change the way that you react to their behavior? Can you look within and see if you did anything to provoke the situation? Can you do anything to fix things? If you think about the way that you normally respond to a difficult interaction with another person, you probably fall into a pattern of thinking:

- It's all their fault.
- It's definitely not my fault.
- Why do they always do this to me?

When you choose to be in one of these mind-sets, there is no room for you to take personal responsibility. You aren't the one to blame, so you don't have to make any changes. But if you think this way, your personal happiness will always be contingent upon the actions of those around you. This irrational belief actually dilutes your power and gives it away. Pretty scary thought, right?

The truth is, you are in charge of how you respond to a situation. Say, for example, that someone cuts you off in traffic. You can choose to become angry and to shout a few choice words out your window as your blood pressure surges up. *Or* you can choose to stay calm and wish the best for that person, for he certainly must be in a hurry for something. You have a **choice.** You are in **control**.

Every moment of every day, you have a chance to ask yourself what you want to think and how you want to feel. Do you want to be happy? Do you want to be sad? Once you understand that you have a choice, you will see how much power you really have. Once you're no longer at the mercy of those around you, you can begin to make decisions that are in *your* best interest. When you make your own choices, when you take control over your own life, that's when happiness starts to blossom.

This doesn't mean it's always easy or that you'll always make the right choice in a given moment. What this does mean, however, is that you become responsible for your own life. Don't give others the power of determining whether or not you will be happy; it's not their job.

Happiness is your job. And it's time to start taking it seriously.

You can take responsibility for your happiness by taking control of your actions and your reactions. And once you do, the world around you will begin to shift. The opportunities for happiness will become tangible because by taking control, you've empowered yourself to embrace them.

Make the choice today. Your happiness is waiting.

Notes to Self:

5. Choice Equals Power

"Okay," you say. *"Lisa, I've come this far. I am beginning to trust what you are telling me about creating happiness in my own life. I guess I will put my faith in you."*

First of all, thank you. Faith is a big deal, and it's something that doesn't come easily for many people, especially when they don't personally know the person they are putting their faith in.

Faith is important. Faith is the condition in which you allow a belief to guide you, even when you have no proof that your thoughts will make any difference in your life. You just have the faith in your heart, and you move in the direction it leads you. It's scary … but it's necessary.

But what does faith have to do with happiness? More than you might realize.

As poet Khalil Gibran once explained,

> *"Faith is a knowledge within the heart, beyond the reach of proof."*

Faith is the fuel that powers the engine of hope. It is your deep, unwavering belief that your hope is connected to the universe and is actually capable of making things happen. If you don't have faith to support your hope, all you are doing is crossing your fingers and wishing for the best. And since our greatest hope in life is for happiness, faith is one of the greatest tools we have to achieve it.

That doesn't mean that having faith will eliminate all fear, nor would we want it to. Fear can be a tremendous motivator and can be used to promote transformation. The problem with fear comes when it paralyzes us, causing us to do nothing with our lives.

All of us have doubts and fears, but we don't have to let them stop us from living the lives we want to live, from doing the things we want to do, or from having the happiness we know we deserve. You deserve to be happy, no matter who you are and no matter what has happened in the past.

Sustainable, authentic happiness is unconditional and can be ongoing in life. It is like a seed that is cultivated and slowly grown over time. You water it, you nurture it, and then you see the plant emerge from the soil. You continue to care for the seed, making sure it has enough sun, enough water, and enough nutrition. And even though that plant might die someday, you know how to grow another.

Unlike happiness, which takes time to cultivate, joy is a far simpler state of being. You don't have to do anything or become anything to experience it. It comes from accepting and embracing what exists in this very moment, for this moment is all that we know and have for sure.

Look around you. Think about your life in this very second. This is what you can count on. Everything can change in an instant; you cannot count on what will happen an hour from now, let alone a day, month, or year. Only now matters. And if that doesn't fill you with wonder, then you need to stop and take stock of how great your life is.

It really is.

Faith and spiritual practice are measures of belief. While you don't have to believe in a certain deity or religious practice in order to have belief, believing in something is important, even if that means you just believe in yourself. Science, however, backs the notion that those having a strong spiritual practice live happier and more fulfilling lives. Connecting to something greater than ourselves invites us to be a part of the universe and not focus myopically on being the center of it. Spiritual practice can take on many forms beyond religion.

Why is it so important to have faith? Because when you have faith in yourself and in the moment you are in, there is nothing you need to fear. Faith is actually the *absence* of fear; it is an inherent acceptance of the present. When you have faith, you can focus on what is before you, and you can react to what you need to react to.

As you read this, where are you now?

Are you are here in the moment, focused? Or are you distracted by the things that surround you? If you are distracted right now, you're not the only one. We live in a society that seeks to distract us each moment of the day.

What could be distracting you from being happy, here and now? Emails, online shopping, social networking—all of these things are just fillers, wasting your time while distracting you from attaining your true happiness.

Turn everything off. Disconnect. Focus on the right here and now and think about what you are feeling. Sometimes, this can be a little too much, which might be why you turn to technology to distract you. When you're distracted, you don't have to think about the right now. You can skip right ahead to the future, or you can think about the past.

Ruminating about history with regret or projecting fear about the future are happiness killers. These actions take you out of the experience you could be having *right now*. The moments we all casually pass up will never happen again. Never. No moment will ever be exactly like this one.

Stop, breathe, and slow down your mind. Remember *where* you are. Remember *who* you are. Think about what you want. Today, you can be happy because you make a choice to be happy. Believe that you are worth the time, the energy, and the effort.

Because you are. Because we all are.

 **Key Five**

It's your own responsibility to be happy.

There's that word again: responsibility. When you think about happiness, the last thing you might think of is the idea of being responsible for it. Isn't happiness something that just occurs?

Not quite.

Even the people in your life who seem to be 100 percent happy are working hard every day to ensure they continue to be that way. True, they might make it look easy, but that is because their choice to be happy is unconscious.

And yours can become that way too.

Let's talk about happiness right now. It may be hard to acknowledge this, but *only you* are responsible for making yourself happy.

Your partner isn't responsible for making you happy. Your friends aren't responsible for making you happy. It's all up to you. And this makes sense, since you're the only one who knows what you need to feel happy. That is, if you've taken the time to discover your happiness.

Figuring out what makes you happy isn't a simple task, especially if up until now you've relied on others or superficial things to make you fleetingly happy. You might have to try out a few different things before you find the recipe for your own personal happiness and contentment.

Begin each day by simply asking yourself what you can do to support your own happiness.

This might include simple things like:

- Engaging in simple pleasures, like making yourself a flavored coffee
- Fitting in a time for meditation
- Going out to exercise
- Making time for a favorite hobby, like playing the piano or taking photographs
- Taking a class, like cooking or sailing
- Considering an alternative career path

In time, you'll begin to see that there are plenty of ways to support your happiness, with simple actions having a very positive effect on you and your life.

But your happiness isn't always going to make everyone happy. At least not at first.

When you begin to take control of your own happiness, you'll notice that your loved ones or colleagues might be confused by the change in your behavior. You're changing the way things have always been, and you might not be meeting the expectations of those around you. By putting yourself and your happiness first, you might have less time to invest in other people's needs and happiness. And you know what? That's okay.

While in the past, you might have focused on trying to make everyone else around you happy, the new you is taking a different approach. And that's a good thing. Because the happier you are, the more you will have to give to others.

What you're doing right now is akin to putting on your own oxygen mask while on an airplane in distress before helping anyone else around you. You can't help others if you don't take care of yourself first.

Of course, it might take time for the people in your life to adjust. Your partner, your friends, and your family might call you selfish for taking time for yourself, for doing things that make you happy. And that's okay. Being selfish is actually okay. Because you're not hurting anyone with the things you're doing. In fact, the better you take care of yourself and your happiness, the better partner, friend, and family member you will be.

If you notice that people around you are having trouble adjusting to your new way of life, it's a good idea to talk to them about why you're doing what you're doing. Most of the time, they'll start to understand once they hear that you're choosing to be happier.

Because who's going to tell you to stop being happy? No one. Happiness, and the quest for sustainable happiness, is contagious. And that, my friend, is why seeking your happiness is in the best interest of your personal community and the world.

When you make changes in your life to invest in your happiness, the people around you will start to wonder what they can do to take responsibility for their happiness, too. And when this happens, when everyone starts taking responsibility for his or her happiness, the joy in the world will grow exponentially. Because happiness is an unlimited resource: as long as we seek happiness in a socially responsible way (without infringing on the happiness of others), there is no limit to what can happen as a result.

Notes to Self:

6. Happiness Creates More Happiness

Happiness used to be something that was hard for you to define. But now, as you've begun to cultivate it, you've felt waves of happiness course through your veins and imbue you with love for your life. Happiness, like love and laughter, is the best medicine.

Who do you love? What do you love? Your partner, your children, your family, your friends, your work, your hobbies, your body, your mind, your gifts as a human? How about yourself, just as you are, and life, just as it is?

Often, we spend a huge amount of time and effort loving other people or things, but we forget that true happiness actually starts with the self. It begins with loving who we are, loving life, and wanting to live life in full bloom, in full-spectrum color, and out loud, while everyone is watching (and even when they're not). And when you love yourself, you will be happier. And when you are happier, the people around you will be happier too.

Because as you now know, happiness creates more happiness. And this is not surprising. A law of physics states that an object in motion will stay in motion until an equal and opposite force acts upon it. This means your happiness will continue to expand, as long as you don't stop it. Your love for life will continue to grow as well—as long as you don't stop that either.

Do you love nature? When are you going out for that hike, stroll, bike ride, or fishing or beach trip?

Do you love to cook? When are you going to plan that special menu, prepare your favorite dish, or create a celebratory environment in which to enjoy this meal?

Do you love your work? When are you going to initiate that passion project you tucked away years ago?

Key Six

Choose to do or include things in your everyday life that make you feel happy.

Your life is filled with places into which you can expand your lessons about love and about happiness. You don't need to hold it back. Happiness isn't something that needs to be limited to how you feel. Love and happiness can be a part of your life, in all of the tasks you handle, mundane though some might seem.

When you begin to realize that happiness creates more happiness, you can see the value of finding happiness in everything that occurs in your life. When you have a happy work life, this will allow you to feel more creative and to be more successful, which encourages you to be happy at home and with your friends, which inspires you to try a new class or a new skill....

Are you starting to see the potential? The possibilities? They are endless.

Every day, do something to make you happy. Prioritize, organize, and execute it. Don't wait until you feel down or sad before you make happiness a priority again. Being happy requires intention and attention. On a daily basis.

Intention is the statement that you want to be happy; you *intend* to be happy in your life. When you state this aloud or to yourself, it becomes a promise you've made to yourself to make changes that will support your intention.

Attention is being aware of the ways that you support—and don't support—your intention. When you focus your attention on your progress, you can make adjustments to the way you live your life to accommodate your intention.

If you want happiness, manifest it with planning. Bring this intention to your attention by taking action. Don't just sit and hope that happiness will show up at your door. Imagine if you wanted to find the love of your life, but you closed yourself off from having a social life by staying home and even avoiding online social networks. That doesn't seem like a good plan, does it?

Do something each day to feed your senses. Read something uplifting. Cater to your inner child by eating dessert first. Listen to beautiful music. Allow yourself to laugh and experience wonder. Nurture your body with healthy food and exercise. Meditate. Feed your mind, body, and spirit.

Sometimes, crystallizing your intention can be accomplished by engaging in a symbolic ritual or act.

For example, take a walk into your backyard and start weeding. As you pull away the pesky weeds and rooted vines that strangle the life out of the precious flowers in your garden, think about the weeds you can pull out of your life. Bad habits, unsupportive friends ... weed them out. Get rid of the guilt, judgment, excuses, and feelings of unworthiness.

Get rid of the feelings that have held you back and that have stopped you from pursuing your true happiness. Get rid of the old stories you have told yourself. Choose to eliminate irrational beliefs and outmoded behaviors.

Each time you see something in your life's garden that doesn't belong, ask yourself what purpose it is serving. If you're not happy with its purpose, remove this belief or situation completely. Take it out by the roots and throw it away.

You're making space for the good things in your life again. Still, it's not enough to just remove the "weeds" that don't serve you. What new things can you plant to contribute to your future happiness?

Here's a simple happiness challenge: set aside one hour a day to do something that makes you happy. One hour may feel like a lot of time, but your well-being is well worth the investment. Sure, we might all say that we're too busy, but that's just an excuse. Because we should always make time for ourselves.

Sow the seeds of joy, cultivate your crops, and take the time to harvest happiness.

Now that you've been working on taking responsibility for your happiness, it's time to start bringing more happiness into your life. Right now. Not tomorrow, not on Monday. Now.

Right now, stop and think about how you're going to fill up that hour you are going to spend on yourself every day. Remember, you don't have to use it all up at once. (For example, it could be fifteen minutes, four times a day.)

Here are some ideas:

- Meditate

- Exercise

- Take a hot bath

- Cook your favorite dish

- Read a book

- Listen to music

- Learn something new

- Play

You get the idea. Think of ways that you can support your happiness every day. Happiness shouldn't be something that you think about once in a while. You need to be more active in your happiness—and that means you need to include something that makes you smile every day.

Some days, it will be easy to find something to do. Other days, you might struggle because you're under a lot of stress, you're sick, or life does what it does best— something you didn't expect.

Even then, find ways to make yourself happy. Even if you worry that others may perceive that what you're doing is silly or strange, do it anyway. This isn't about them or their judgment. This is about you and your happiness. If you feel like wearing a cocktail dress or tuxedo to lunch because it makes you feel glamorous or suave, do it. If you want to take up line dancing or ballet at the age of forty-six, do it. If you want to write a screenplay (even though you have zero experience), do it. If it makes you smile, don't question it. *Do it.*

This isn't about asking others to define your happiness. This is about *you* and you alone. What can you do each day to make yourself as happy as possible?

Now do it. I know you want to.

Notes to Self:

7. The H-Factor challenge

The funny thing about happiness is that it is not about control. It is about consciously turning on your own internal lights and shining them out into the world to illuminate what is positive and right within your immediate universe.

Happiness begins when you admit to yourself that you deserve happiness, in whatever form that makes the most sense to you. While you might think you understand happiness right now, it's your commitment to the "H-Factor" (the Happiness Factor, that is) that adds up to lifelong happiness and joy. You ask, *What is this H-Factor*? The H-Factor is simple: it is that which brings us happiness, increases our joy, helps us find our smiles, and makes our hearts sing. It is **not** the yellow smiley face that is often an annoying symbol of fleeting/temporal happiness. We embody the "H-Factor" when we find ourselves enraptured by the moment we are in, without regard to time, space, or external circumstances. It exists when we are in flow with our lives and are aware of how good it feels.

For my thesis project in graduate school, I traveled around the world with my daughter, Kayla, to explore my hypothesis that every person, regardless of socioeconomic level, age, ethnicity, career, health, or life circumstances, possesses happiness or the means to feel happy. Together, we interviewed people from all walks of life—from religious leaders, politicians, inmates, and actors to street vendors and the homeless—in an effort to discover the universal keys to happiness. The tangible result was my film, *H-Factor...Where Is Your Heart?* The more profound result was watching the change in my daughter, in the people we interviewed, and in me when happiness became the subject of the conversation instead of a by product or afterthought.

Even though you now understand what the H-Factor is, it doesn't reside where you may think.

- **Can you discover the secret to the H-Factor in the latest self-help guide or by going to a therapist?**

No, the H-Factor is not contained in any self-help book. Not even this one. It's also not about processing negative emotions or past traumas; it's not about what your parents did or did not do.

- **Will you discover the H-Factor if you cleanse all the toxins out of your body?**

No. You may feel better physically after a cleanse, but the H-Factor has nothing to do with a high colonic or juice fast.

- **Can a guru or teacher provide you with the keys to the big H-Factor secret by unlocking the mysticism and magic of the universe?**

No. That would be moving in the wrong direction. The H-Factor isn't in the far reaches of the universe; it is in **you**.

You are the light. The secret to happiness resides within you. It is already there—just flip the switch and turn up the brilliance. Feelings of depression, oppression, and suppression are all a manifestation of repressing the light of joy within you. We came into the world happy and then the light within us was tarnished by experience. In order to rekindle the light within, we must reawaken our inherent nature.

Repression is part of the compression that limits our brilliance. When we live in a contracted state, we are coiled up and closed off from life. Conversely, when we live in an open state of mind and being, our consciousness expands. Your happiness already exists; just let it shine.

Key Seven

Treat yourself with honor, grace, kindness, integrity, and self-love.

The trick is learning to embrace "In-Joyment." Your joy is already inside you. True happiness comes from within. When you treat yourself with the respect you deserve, you will attract the happiness you deserve. The only way to cultivate the light that is within you is to treat yourself with honor, with grace, with kindness, with integrity, and with self-love.

What does this look like?

- Make promises to yourself that you can keep.
- Do things that you actually want to do that serve your growth.
- Be kind to your body and your spirit.
- Surround yourself with positive people.
- Remember your happiness first.
- Consider the feelings of others.
- Align your actions with your needs.

When you move through each day, you will move differently if you're happy. The moment you realize that you are the one who is responsible for your happiness, that you deserve happiness, and that you *are* happiness, you'll treat yourself better and authentically feel more joyful. You will experience, in a word, "In-Joyment."

Starting right now, right here, accept nothing less than the best for yourself. How you define this is up to you. For example, if you're asked to go to a certain event and you really do not want to go, say no instead of yes (as you might have done in the past).

When you listen to yourself and treat yourself with respect, you will notice that you are better able to care for yourself and meet your needs. You already do this for everyone around you. Why not for yourself? Besides, the better you care for yourself, the more you will have to give to your friends, family, and the world at large.

Take the H-Factor challenge and treat yourself the way you deserve to be treated. It's the only way to tap into your inner light.

Notes to Self:

8. Getting It And Keeping It

Each day, you get to make a decision: to be happy or not to be happy. You have the freedom to be joyful or the liberty to be miserable. Instead of feeling like you are a victim in your own life, you have learned that you are the one who calls the shots, the one who directs the traffic in your mind, and the one who creates happiness. You are, in fact, your own hero.

When you are active in creating happiness, things can go well. But because you've had many years of feeling that everyone else is to blame for your bad days, it might be easy (at first) to slip back into your old ways.

Key Eight

Being mindful that what you are doing allows you to correct your course on the way to happiness. Happiness is an inside job. Happiness is *your* inside job.

Promise yourself right now that you will become aware of negative thoughts when they creep in. Notice when you're not as happy as you would like, and ask yourself these questions:

- What am I feeling right now?

- What am I doing that isn't supporting my happiness?

- What action will I take to support my happiness?

These questions will put you back on track, and they will allow you to refocus your mind on what is positive and what is possible in your life.

The more you question what you're doing and how you're moving through your life, the more aware you will become of the times when you need to make a change to better support your happiness.

Every day is a lesson, and every day is an opportunity. How will you choose to show up for life?

Creating Your Happiness First-Aid Kit

As you've seen so far, happiness isn't elusive. It isn't something that hides in the ether, waiting for you to accidentally stumble upon it. It is a choice. It is a way of life. And it can be harnessed using the steps we've already talked about. But sometimes, you need more than just a mental checklist of happiness theories. You need concrete reminders to help you connect with your happiness. Don't worry. I've got you covered. All you need is a Happiness First-Aid Kit, filled with everyday objects to guide you back to your happiness if you ever lose your way.

To create your Happiness First-Aid Kit, you'll need:

- **Mirror**: to remind you that the change starts from within.

- **Chocolate**: to remind you to eat dessert first—don't postpone your joy.

- **Bubbles**: to remind you to connect to your inherent childlike sense of wonder to stimulate curiosity, enchantment, and delight.

- **Rose-Colored Glasses**: to remind you that the way we view the world governs our attitudes and actions.

- **Package of Kool-Aid**: to remind you that pure belief, a leap of faith, is the sweet elixir of self-mastery. Sometimes, we have to fake it until we make it.

- **Balloon**: to remind you that we all have to expel our hot air from time to time.

- **Candle**: to remind you of the light we all have within us.

- **A Packet of Seeds**: to remind you that we can choose to cultivate joy at any time by planting the seeds, watering, and nurturing our personal well-being crop.

Once you gather your happiness symbols, put your Happiness First-Aid Kit somewhere you can see it regularly. Create a special box or pouch to hold these and other meaningful symbols. When you feel like you're veering off your happiness path, peek into your kit and find the remedy. Of course, a Happiness First-Aid Kit is a personal thing, so feel free to add to it.

So you have your Keys. You have your Happiness First-Aid Kit. You are well on your way to living a happier, more fulfilling life. But there's one more thing I can do for you: I'm going to give you five basic things you can implement on a daily basis to make sure you—and your happiness—flourish.

The Not-So-Secret "H" Secrets

1. **Stay out of your own way.** Negative self-talk, doubt, judgment, fear, anxiety, and unforgiving behaviors are all spirit-killers and happiness-dampeners. When these feelings creep up, make a conscious effort to turn them off. Instead, believe in yourself. The universe will follow suit.

2. **Appreciate what is right in life, while minimizing what is wrong.** Find the good in your life and exalt it. Express gratitude. Don't waste your strength envying others for what they have and you don't. Be joyful for another's bliss, as you would for your own.

3. **Surround yourself with happy people.** Happiness is positively viral and has a domino effect.

4. **Smile and make eye contact with others.** Connect with the universe. Let the world know your lights are on. Even if you don't see a smile on people's faces, give them yours.

5. **Pay it forward.** Do something nice for someone else. Try putting a few coins in a stranger's expired parking meter. Buy a cup of coffee for the person behind you in line at the café. Practice random acts of kindness, and you'll expand your joy and the joy of those around you.

You have a plan! You have some skills to use. Are you feeling happier?

Happiness is like a muscle. If we don't use it, we will lose it. We're all hard-wired to exist, but we're not necessarily wired to be happy. The good news is we can train for greater joy through using good tools and practice. Happiness can be cultivated.

If you think about it, we don't need to be happy in order to survive. And we're animals, so survival is the most important thing, above all else. But surviving is different than thriving. And happiness is the potion that allows us to thrive physically, mentally, emotionally, and spiritually.

And that's why we need to refine our skills, because happiness takes practice. First, figure out what makes you happy. Next, forget about what others may think. And third, invest in your happiness with your time, your spirit, and your light.

Remember to keep practicing your happiness skills so they don't get rusty. In the hustle and bustle of life, it's easy to let your happiness take a backseat to your busy schedule and obligations. If you don't practice happiness, your capacity for happiness will suffer, like muscles that atrophy without use. By practicing your happiness, you will nourish your mind, your body, and your spirit, and as a result, every facet of your life will benefit.

Many of us are worried about not being happy—but not many of us do something about it. That's because we look at happiness as something that is elusive and defined by fate. It's not. Happiness is a skill, a skill we can all develop. It's not something that's out of reach. Far from it. Happiness is something that you can learn, something you can refine, and something that you can *master*.

Recapping the Eight Keys to Unlocking a Joyful Life:

Key One: Life is tough, but happiness is available to all.

Key Two: Your inner child is your inner sage.

Key Three: More is not always better.

Key Four: We cannot control life, only ourselves.

Key Five: Our happiness is our personal responsibility.

Key Six: Choose activities and people that foster happiness.

Key Seven: Treat yourself the way you wish to be treated.

Key Eight: Happiness is an inside job. Happiness is *your* inside job.

You see, happiness is our birthright, but not our entitlement. Each of us came into the world happy. It is human nature. Entitled to be happy? Who said? Entitlements are for those of us who believe we are owed something. Some outside source does not grant happiness to us. Happiness is ours to claim at any time and any place, regardless of external circumstance.

Notes to Self:

Afterword

My question to you, dear reader, is what will you do with these keys to your kingdom of greater happiness and well-being? Consider spreading joy to others who could really use it now!

Each week I have the greater honor of hosting *Harvesting Happiness Talk Radio*. The show profiles amazing people living their dreams and serving others to help maximize their human potential. I close each episode with the following parting thoughts:

Happiness is not a destination. It cannot be bought, sold, or traded. Happiness will never invite you to the party. Happiness simply comes down to a choice to show up, each and every day, in the world with passion, purpose, place, and meaning. How are you going to choose to show up for life? Wishing you kind thoughts, kinder words, and the kindest actions.

Looking for another way to receive and give happiness? Consider this:

Harvesting Happiness for Heroes, a pending 501(c)(3) non profit corporation dedicated to serving warriors who have served our country. Your donations support our mission to offer stigma-free, positive psychology coaching services to our returning war veterans and their loved ones who are experiencing combat trauma and other post-deployment reintegration issues, to reawaken joy in their hearts and minds. Remember, happiness is not about politics. Happiness is about paying it forward and fueling the word's joy reserve. Join me in helping those who have selflessly served us.

Until next time ... remember that happiness is an inside job. Happiness is your inside job.

For more information about how you can get involved in supporting our warriors, please visit www.HH4Heroes. org. To learn more about Lisa and her work, please visit www.harvestinghappiness.com or download free podcasts of Harvesting Happiness Talk Radio *show on* iTunes.

A Happiness Is An Inside Job™ Training Tool

Acknowledgments

Gratitude unlocks the fullness of life. It turns what we have into enough, and more. It turns denial into acceptance, chaos to order, confusion to clarity. It can turn a meal into a feast, a house into a home, a stranger into a friend. Gratitude makes sense of our past, brings peace for today, and creates a vision for tomorrow.

— *Melody Beattie*

We know it takes a village to help raise a child. It takes an army to bring any worthwhile project to fruition. I have been blessed with many Warriors of Joy helping to support my happiness initiatives through film, felicitation, and philanthropy.

There is a long list of people to thank for their help, encouragement, and steadfast belief in me. Thank you to all who have stood with me through the creative process: my family, friends, coworkers, teachers, mentors, and fellow "felicitators," whose own eyes were opened wide along the way.

With heartfelt gratitude to my parents, Sharon, Bob, Karen, and Dennis; my "was-band" Michael, who unwittingly helped me find my smile; my siblings, Erin, Rory, Scott, and their families, who keep on loving no matter what; and my behind-the-scenes Warriors of Joy support team: Sandra Beck, Dr. Robert Biswas-Diener, also known as the Indiana Jones of Positive Psychology, Larry Broughton, Sophie Chi, Phil Dyer, Jill Ettinger, Melody Godfred, Carrie Hill, Brigitte Huff, Robin Boyd January, Dr. Lynn Johnson, Langdon Street Press, Hannah Lee, Joody Marks, Jill Martin, John Martin, Keri Martin, Lisa (Mighty-Girl) Mendell, Brandon Na, Heather Pilz, Marna Poole, Jared Rosen, Joni Sand, Steven Shaps, Kelly St. Clair, Rich Tamayo, Toginet Radio, Roz Walker, Dustin Zahn, and Drs. Ron and Mary Hulnick of the University of Santa Monica, who dared the class of 2007 not to live a "chicken shit" life. I know I did not disappoint you. Thank you for all of the gifts you have given me.

No doubt there are people I have forgotten to include here, but that's simply because my brain has temporarily frozen, not because you aren't deeply appreciated and admired for your gifts.

With deep appreciation for those forces seen and unseen who challenge me to be my best, each and every day.

With heartfelt gratitude and in happiness,

Lisa

About the Author

Lisa Cypers Kamen is an internationally recognized happiness expert. Ms. Kamen is acclaimed for her engaging blend of positive and spiritual psychology coaching, workshops, and philanthropic projects. Through her books, radio show, media appearances, and inspiring documentary films, such as *H Factor...Where Is Your Heart?*, Ms. Kamen serves to educate, facilitate happiness, and cultivate greater well-being in private and public audiences around the world. Ms. Kamen recently launched Harvesting Happiness for Heroes, a pending 501(c)(3) non-profit corporation dedicated to bringing integrated psychology coaching tools and mindfulness training to Veterans and their loved ones challenged by combat trauma and other post-deployment reintegration issues. Ms. Kamen is regularly featured for her work, including on *The Huffington Post*, ABC and CBS television, *Yahoo!* News, and "Money Watch." She completed her master's degree in spiritual psychology at the University of Santa Monica and resides in Southern California with her two children.

FILMOGRAPHY - How do we find, cultivate and sustain happiness in an increasingly busy and complicated world? Lisa Cypers Kamen, MA spiritual psychology, and her young daughter, Kayla, explore the very serious business of happiness through their documentary film, *H-Factor...Where Is Your Heart?* This film is a journey of the human spirit that educates, delights, provokes, and empowers well-being to skeptics and seekers of any age.

www.whatisyourhappiness.com

WWW.WHATISYOURHAPPINESS.COM

FELICITATION - Creating a wonderful life does not happen by accident. Living a happy life comes from the conscious choices we make everyday– even the smallest adjustment can have the largest impact. Our coaching programs can assist you in identifying and creating the fulfilling life you want. You can cultivate greater mental, physical, and emotional patterns to release you from being stuck and assist you in establishing and acheiving your goals. Discover and harvest Positive Psychology tools for enjoying life more fully through greater self-mastery. Sample Harvesting Happiness on our free weekly talk radio show with downloadable podcasts that explores the art of human flourishing.

www.harvestinghappiness.com

WWW.HARVESTINGHAPPINESS.COM

PHILANTHROPY - Our mission objective is to offer stigma-free support services to returning military personnel and their loved ones challenged by combat trauma and other post-deployment reintegration issues. We offer Battle Buddy workshops, family awareness training, online community support, one-on-one coaching services, as well as retreats for Warriors to decompress from battle to learn the tools available for them to adapt their military skills to civilian society while reawakening joy in their hearts and minds. HH4Heroes is a pending 501(c)(3) non profit corporation.

www.hh4heroes.org

HARVESTING **FⓞR HEROES** HAPPINESS
HARVESTING HAPPINESS FOR HEROES WWW.HH4HEROES.ORG

HAPPINESS IS AN INSIDE JOB!™